CLARK GABLE

A Hollywood Portrait

CLARK GABLE

A Hollywood Portrait

Marie Cahill

SMITHMARK

This edition published in 1992
by SMITHMARK Publishers Inc.,
112 Madison Avenue,
New York, New York 10016.

SMITHMARK books are available for bulk purchase for sales promotion and premium use. For details write or telephone the Manager of Special Sales, SMITHMARK Publishers Inc., 112 Madison Avenue, New York, NY 10016. (212) 532-6600.

Produced by Brompton Books Corp.,
15 Sherwood Place,
Greenwich, CT 06830.

ISBN 0-8317-4602-5

Printed in Hong Kong

10 9 8 7 6 5 4 3 2 1

All photos courtesy of American Graphic Systems Archives.

Dedication: To my mother, whose heart still flutters when she sees a picture of Clark Gable.

Page 1: Clark Gable during the early years at MGM, the foremost studio during Hollywood's Golden Age. His career with MGM spanned a quarter of a century.
Page 2: The first of the he-man heros, Gable appealed to men as well as women.
Facing page: To millions of movie lovers, Clark Gable was the King of Hollywood, but he thought of himself as 'a lucky guy from Ohio who happened to be in the right place at the right time.'

INTRODUCTION

Clark Gable—the King of Hollywood—was a man's man and a woman's dream. An enduring star for 30 years, Gable's name was synonymous with virility and sex appeal.

Clark Gable was born William Clark Gable in Cadiz, Ohio on 1 February 1901. His mother died when he was young and his father later remarried. Gable quit school at 14 to work in a tire factory in nearby Akron. While living

Below: William Clark Gable, age 18 months.

Facing page: An early publicity still from MGM.

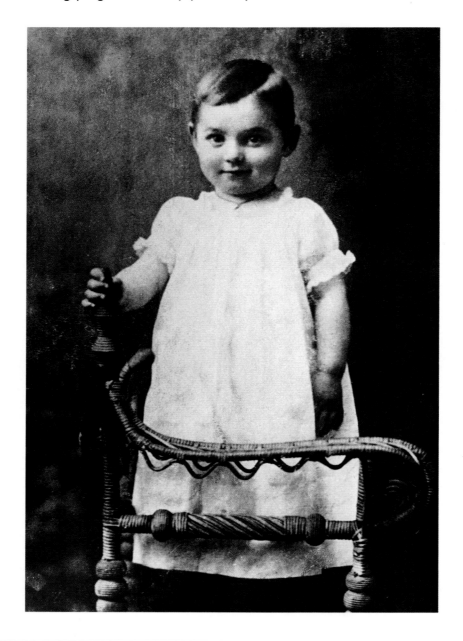

there, he saw his first play and was so enthralled with the theater that he started working for free as a call boy backstage. Just when he was given the opportunity to play a few bit parts, his father, an oil driller, moved to Oklahoma, taking the boy with him. Gable worked the oil fields with his father until he was 21 and a traveling troupe came through town.

His travels took him to Oregon, where he moved from job to job—as a lumberjack and a tie salesman, among other things—until another acting troupe came along. Josephine Dillon, the lead actress with the troupe, took the young actor under her wing. Her interest in Gable went beyond professional courtesy, and when the troupe landed in Hollywood in 1924, Dillon and Gable were married. He was 23; she was 37.

For a brief time, Gable worked as an extra in such films as Lubitsch's **Forbidden Paradise** (1924) and Von Stroheim's **The Merry Widow** (1925). When his career stalled, Gable left Hollywood *and* his wife and went on the road with touring stage companies. On Broadway, he landed the romantic lead in **Machinal** in 1928. Two years later he starred opposite Alice Brady in **Love, Honor and Obey**, a part which led to the leading role in the Los Angeles production of **The Last Mile** (1930). Lionel Barrymore, a costar from the road production, recognized

Above: Gable with Shirley Temple, Mickey Rooney and Judy Garland at MGM Studios. In 1934, Rooney had appeared with Gable in **Manhattan Melodrama**, playing Gable's character (Blackie Gallagher) as a child. Judy Garland voiced everyone's feelings for the King of Hollywood when she sang 'Dear Mr Gable—You Made Me Love You' in **Broadway Melody of 1938**.

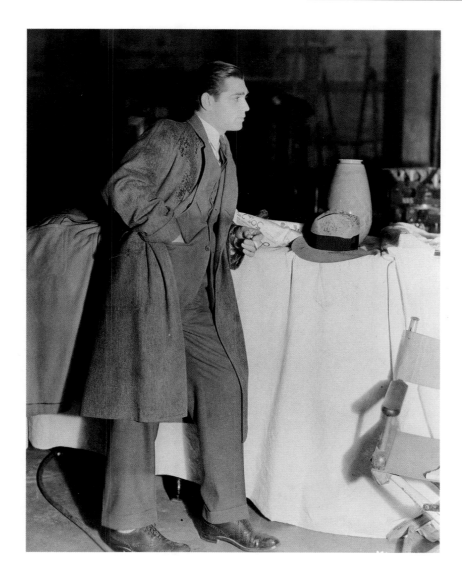

Gable's talent and persuaded MGM to give him a screen test. The studio was not impressed. Gable received a similar reaction at Warner Bros, where Darryl F Zanuck declared: 'His ears are too big. He looks like an ape.'

By this time, Gable was divorced from Josephine Dillon and married to Ria Langham, a Texas socialite who was 17 years older than he was.

In 1931, with the help of an agent, Gable finally landed the part of the villain in **The Painted Desert**, a western directed by William Boyd, and soon made a name for himself playing rough and rugged characters. The turning point in his career was a supporting role in **A Free Soul** (1931), which found him pushing Norma Shearer around. Audiences responded to Gable's brutish virility and he quickly became a leading man at MGM. By year's end, he had starred in a dozen films.

It was Clark Gable's performance as the wise-cracking reporter in Frank Capra's **It Happened One Night** (1934) that earned him an Academy Award and secured his fame as an actor. Ironically, he had resisted the part, which had been doled out to him as punishment for complaining about being typecast as a brute.

From there Gable's star continued to rise, and he was dubbed 'The King' of Hollywood. In 1939, he was cast in **Gone With the Wind** as the dashing Rhett Butler, the role for which he is best remembered. In order to procure Gable for

Above: Clark Gable, relaxing between takes.

the film, producer David O Selznick agreed to pay MGM a share of the profits, but the price was worth it, because Gable, as expected, had audiences flocking to see **Gone With the Wind**.

While filming **Gone With the Wind**, Gable divorced his second wife and married his third, actress Carole Lombard. The marriage between the glamorous, sophisticated come- dienne and the King of Hollywood was considered a 'match made in Heaven.' Sadly, their happiness was short-lived. While on a war bond drive, Carole Lombard was killed in a plane crash. A grief-stricken Gable temporarily gave up acting for real-life heroics and joined the Army during World War II. He flew several bombing missions over Ger- many and was awarded the Distinguished Flying Cross and the Air Medal.

Gable's much-anticipated return to Hollywood in **Adven- ture** (1945) was heralded by the slogan: 'Gable's Back, and Garson's Got Him.' Still suffering from Lombard's death, he gained weight and began drinking heavily. In 1949, Gable married Lady Sylvia Ashley, a former actress with an uncanny resemblance to Carole Lombard, but the mar- riage lasted less than two years. He married again in 1955, this time to Kay Spreckels, another blonde in the Lombard mold. The marriage was a happy one, enduring until Gable's death.

When his contract with MGM came up for renewal in 1954, it was not renewed so Gable started his own produc- tion company, Gabco. He finished off the decade with several films to his credit, none particularly memorable. However, his final film, **The Misfits** (1961) received consid- erable acclaim, though he did not live to hear his rave reviews. The filming had been a grueling experience. Though he was now nearly 60, he insisted on doing his own stunts. Gable suffered a heart attack and died on 16 November 1960. The following March his only child and much longed for son, John Clark, was born.

At the time of his death, Clark Gable was still the undis- puted King of Hollywood, but his Kingdom's Golden Age had passed and there was no heir to take his place.

Facing page and above: Publicity stills like these of Clark Gable were as important to an actor's career as the charac- ters they played.

CLARK GABLE

Gable did a screen test for a role in Warner Bros' **Little Caesar**, but the studio heads rejected him, declaring Gable ugly and a big ape. MGM, at the urging of Lionel Barrymore, had Gable do two screen tests before signing him to a short-term contract at $350 a week. Audiences, however, had no such hesitation. The more they saw of Gable, the more they wanted. Clark Gable (*above*) signing an autograph.

Facing page: A publicity still for **A Free Soul** (1931). Up to this point, Gable had had supporting roles in a half a dozen films. Still playing the second in **A Free Soul**, he stole the show from leading players Norma Shearer, Leslie Howard and Lionel Barrymore. Audiences loved him and MGM responded with a barrage of publicity for its hottest new star.

Above: This still captures Gable looking relaxed behind the scenes. Gable always seemed at ease and so sure of himself. His image of self-assurance and masculinity made him the quintessential American movie star.

Facing page: Gable — now a leading man — relaxing on the set of **Strange Interlude** in 1932. The previous year had been a hectic one for Gable. He had started the year as a bit player and by year's end, with a dozen films to his credit, he had skyrocketed to fame.

Facing page and above: As Hollywood made the transition from silent films to talkies, MGM desperately needed a leading male star, as all of the studio's top stars were female—Greta Garbo, Joan Crawford, Norma Shearer. Clark Gable fit the bill.

Above: Gable and his second wife, Ria Langham, a wealthy Texas socialite. The two met in 1928 when Gable was appearing with a stock company in Houston.

Facing page: Gable on the MGM lot in the early 1930s.

Left: Clark Gable with Norma Shearer and Leslie Howard in **A Free Soul** (1931). Gable's seventh film, **A Free Soul** was the one that helped create the virile, he-man image for which Gable is famous. At first it seemed that this would be another routine gangster role.

Norma Shearer, at the time Hollywood's reigning leading lady, plays Jan, the daughter of alcoholic lawyer Stephen Ashe (Lionel Barrymore). Through her father, Jan meets Ace Wilfong (Clark Gable), a gambler and underworld leader. She dumps her fiancé (Leslie Howard) and becomes Ace's lover. Jan is no gangster's moll—she's rich, headstrong. A free soul, she does exactly what she wants. Her father disapproves and promises to give up drinking if she will give up Ace. She agrees, but her father can't keep up his end of the bargain, and she goes back to Ace, who has turned into a brute.

The public was ready for a new type of leading man. Perhaps it was a reaction to the times, but whatever the cause, it was not lost on Howard Strickling of the MGM publicity department that the days of the romantic, genteel leading man were over. Strickling promoted the idea of a new kind of hero, and audiences loved it when Gable pushed his leading lady around. Norma Shearer later said, 'It was Clark who made villains popular. Instead of the audience wanting the good guy to get the girl, they wanted the heavy to win her.'

Most of the critics praised Barrymore, who won an Oscar for his performance. Gable's role was dismissed as relatively unimportant. The fans, however, went wild, writing fan letters to him and to MGM, demanding more Gable. MGM responded by tearing up Gable's contract and writing a new one for $1150 a week.

Gable had arrived.

Right: The camera zooms in for a close-up of Gable. With each successive movie, more and more letters poured into MGM about 'that handsome young actor,' and the studio began to shape the Clark Gable image. Howard Strickling, Gable's publicist and good friend, was immediately struck by Gable's physical presence and natural charm. He saw Gable as a real he-man and honed that image for the public.

In reality the image was not far from the truth, for Gable did have the perfect background for the he-man image, having worked as a lumberman and oiler. Gable wasn't yet the sportsman but once introduced to hunting and fishing he found he was in his element.

Soon publicity shots of Gable featured him on horseback, surrounded by fishing reels or guns, or leaning casually against a sporty roadster. Gable fit into his image naturally. He liked it, and so did the public.

Suddenly, Gable was a hot property. Strickling and the publicity department were overwhelmed by requests for information on Gable. In those days, studios were cautious and kept close watch over their stables of stars. MGM was worried that word of Gable's first marriage would create a scandal but eventually the studio decided to turn the press loose on Gable. What everyone discovered was that Clark Gable was just a regular guy.

MGM had opened a can of worms that it hadn't bargained on: Gable wasn't scandalous; he was boring. From then on, MGM decided that Gable should go hunting or fishing between films. That suited Clark Gable just fine.

While on a hunting trip, Gable read that he was to star with Greta Garbo in her next picture, **Susan Lenox—Her Fall and Rise** (1931). To be teamed with the great Garbo (*these pages*) was a triumph for Gable, though he was naturally frustrated that he hadn't been consulted about the part. Such were the ways of studio contracts.

As it turned out, the chemistry between the two stars was never quite right. Though Garbo received stunning reviews, the part was ill-suited for Gable—something that should have been indicated by the train of 22 writers that worked on the film. Filming dragged on for 49 days (compared to the usual 35), and Garbo walked off the set six times. It was the one and only film Gable and Garbo did together, and he was relieved when it was all over. Nevertheless, working with Garbo had its advantages. The film did well at the box office, which made MGM happy.

These pages: Clark Gable and one of his 'leading' leading ladies of the 1930s, Joan Crawford. The two starred in six films together, the first of which was **Dance, Fools, Dance** (1931), which was based on the shooting of Jake Lingle and the St Valentine's Day Massacre. During filming, Joan discovered what the rest of Hollywood was about to: Gable had presence. In her autobiography, Crawford recalled a scene from the film in which he grabbed her and threatened the life of her brother: 'His nearness had such impact, my knees buckled. If he hadn't held me by both shoulders, I'd have dropped.'

While they were filming **Possessed** (1931), rumors circulated that they were having an affair. 'In the picture, we were madly in love,' Joan wrote. 'When the scenes ended, the emotions didn't.' At the time, Clark was married to Ria; he had in fact just married her again because the legality of the original ceremony was questionable. Joan's marriage to Douglas Fairbanks, Jr was all but over, and the Hollywood oddsmakers figured the glamorous star as an easy bet to woo Gable from his wife. MGM, however, wanted no such scandal. Perhaps pressure from the studio did cool the flames of passion. At any rate, Joan settled for friendship rather than marriage.

After **Possessed**, MGM immediately put Gable to work on **Hell Divers** (1931), the saga of naval aviators. Gable is seen *above* with Marjorie Rambeau, who played a minor role. **Hell Divers** was billed as a man's movie—lots of action, with a hint of romance for good measure. Dorothy Jordan as Ann, Gable's girl friend, provided the romantic element, but her part was over before the film was. The film also featured Marie Prevost and Conrad Nagel.

Hell Divers paired Wallace Beery (*above*) as Windy with Gable as Steve. A barroom brawl between the two heightens an already intense rivalry and fills Windy, the loser, with an intense hatred for his fellow officer. Windy gets even by creating trouble between Steve and his girl friend. Goodness triumphs in the end when Windy gives his life to rescue Steve, whose plane has crashed.

Critics cheered Beery's performance, but not much else about the move, a sentiment that was shared by Gable himself. Beery was MGM's highest paid actor at the time, even though Gable was one of Hollywood's biggest box office draws. Gable was naturally disturbed by this inequity. He wanted a higher salary and a much-needed vacation. MGM did give him a new contract, but instead of a vacation Gable reported to work for **Polly of the Circus** (1932).

These pages: Publicity stills for **Red Dust**, Gable's big hit of 1932. He didn't care for the shot on the *facing page* because he didn't like the way it showed his ears. Photographer Clarence Bull assured Gable that if Valentino's nostrils could become sex symbols, so could Gable's ears.

Right: **Red Dust** once again teamed Clark Gable with Jean Harlow, the original blonde bombshell. The two had previously starred together in **The Secret Six** (1931), but that earlier association lacked the sexual firepower of **Red Dust**.

As Dennis Carson, the boss of a rubber plantation, Gable's he-man image was solidified. He spends a good part of the film sweaty and unshaven and even takes a bullet from disgruntled lover, Mary Astor. As the wise-cracking prostitute who wins the man in the end, Harlow was lusty and clearly enjoyed sex, while Gable clearly enjoyed her. Audiences were both shocked and amused by the scene in which Gable finds her bathing in a rain barrel.

For its day, **Red Dust** was quite erotic, combining Gable's virility with Harlow's lusty charm. Yet the film squeaked by the censorial Hays Office because it broke no specific rules. As funny as it was sexy, **Red Dust** highlighted Harlow's comedic skills and made excellent use of Gable as straight man.

Their passionate onscreen relationship ignited the usual rumors of an affair, but in this case the rumors were nothing more than rumors. Never lovers, the two were very close, lifelong friends.

Above: In **The White Sister** (1933), Gable played opposite Helen Hayes.

Facing page: Gable and Norma Shearer in **Strange Interlude** (1932), the second of their three films together.

These pages: Clark Gable first met Carole Lombard on the set of **No Man of Her Own** (1932), a lighthearted comedy about a card shark (Gable) who marries a smalltown beauty (Lombard) on a bet and then falls in love with her.

Carole Lombard made her screen debut at the age of 13 in **A Perfect Crime** (1921). After she completed her education, she returned to Hollywood, eventually becoming one of Mack Sennett's bathing beauties. Sennett's silent two-reelers helped her develop her trademark screwball style. With the advent of sound, Carole signed with Paramount about the same time that Gable signed with MGM. Carole was ambitious, professional and a practical joker. Within a few short years of signing with Paramount, this zany and brilliant comedienne would become one of the highest paid female movie stars and, in one of Hollywood's most magical love stories, the wife of Clark Gable.

At the time of **No Man of Her Own**, however, Carole was married to William Powell and found Clark Gable to be stuffy, while he thought her too boisterous. Four years later their feelings would change when they met once again at a Hollywood bash.

These pages: Clark Gable and Jean Harlow were reunited in **Hold Your Man** (1933), a melodrama featuring Gable as a con man and Harlow as Ruby, the woman who loves him. After a series of tangled schemes, Ruby ends up in reform school, taking the rap for Eddie (Gable) who accidently killed a man. Eddie has flown the coop, but when he learns that Ruby is pregnant, he returns to marry her.

Overleaf: Moments after Eddie has married Ruby, the police arrive on the scene and take him away. Thanks to a clever lawyer, he gets off easy and soon joins his waiting wife and baby son. He tells her he is going straight, and they head for Cincinnati, where a job and respectability await them.

678-x-1

Above: Clark Gable and one of his favorite leading ladies, Jean Harlow, in **Hold Your Man**. Harlow's career began in earnest after she signed with MGM in 1932. Her vibrant personality made her one of Hollywood's best loved stars.

Facing page: With Jean Harlow behind the scenes of **Hold Your Man** (1933). Based on a story by Anita Loos, **Hold Your Man** was directed by Sam Wood, who would later be called in to assist director Victor Fleming on **Gone with the Wind** (1939).

These pages: Two studies of Clark Gable from a series of 1934 portraits by Clarence Sinclair Bull, one of Hollywood's masters.

Above: A publicity still for **It Happened One Night** (1934). Gable starred with Claudette Colbert (*previous pages*) in this delightful Frank Capra comedy. Colbert plays Ellie, an heiress who is running away from her tycoon father. As she boards a bus she meets Peter, a reporter (Gable), who has just been fired. Since they each have limited funds, the two decide to pool their resources.

It Happened One Night was the big winner at the 1934 Academy Awards ceremony, garnering Best Picture, Best Actor, Best Actress, Best Director and Best Adaptation. Thirty-five years would pass before another film would take as many top awards (Patton in 1970), and it wasn't until 1975 that a costarring actor and actress would again win simultaneous Oscars (Jack Nicholson and Louise Fletcher in **One Flew Over the Cuckoos Nest**).

It was Gable's one and only Academy Award. Ironically, he had been angry about doing the picture, which Louis Mayer doled out to him as a disciplinary action.

Facing page: Gable and costar Constance Bennett in **After Office Hours** (1935). Four years earlier the two had appeared in **The Easiest Way** (1931), but she had been the leading lady while Gable was at the bottom of the cast list.

Above: Gable with Movita, in **Mutiny on the Bounty** (1935). He had originally objected to the role, fearing that appearing in knickers and a ponytail would damage his image. Later Gable would admit that he had been wrong about the film, which he came to regard as one of his favorites: 'It was something you could get your teeth into, for it was history, a story about the struggle of real men, without the usual load of cinema romance.'

Gable's outstanding performance as Fletcher Christian earned him a nomination for an Academy Award and helped him make his mark as a dramatic actor.

Left: Another winning Gable picture for 1935 was **China Seas**, with Jean Harlow and Wallace Beery. The *New York Times* proclaimed Gable outstanding, adding 'It is a role which demands vigor, an infectious, devil-may-care philosophy and the stinging passion of distempered blood, and while Gable has displayed these qualities before, it is one of his most convincing portrayals.'

Right and overleaf: The making of **China Seas** (1935). Gable plays the captain of a ship bound for Hong Kong with a shipment of gold. To complicate matters for Captain Alan Gaskell (Gable), his fiancée, Sybil (Rosalind Russell), and his mistress, China Doll (Jean Harlow), are both on board.

China Doll is heartbroken when she learns of Gaskell's engagement and consequently gets mixed up with James MacArdle, an unscrupulous trader played by Wallace Beery. Suspecting that MacArdle is out to steal the gold, she waits in Gaskell's quarters to warn him. He misinterprets her reason for being there and orders her out. Angered by Gaskell's summary dismissal, China Doll decides to aid MacArdle. Meanwhile, pirates board the ship and torture Gaskell, who refuses to tell them where the gold is hidden.

Everything ends happily in this action-filled romance. The pirates are stopped, MacArdle's plot is thwarted and Gaskell realizes that China Doll is his one true love.

Gable took the he-man image seriously for this film, refusing to let the stunt men take his place during dangerous shots. And when Gable made up his mind that he was going to do something, there was nothing director Tay Garnett could do to stop him.

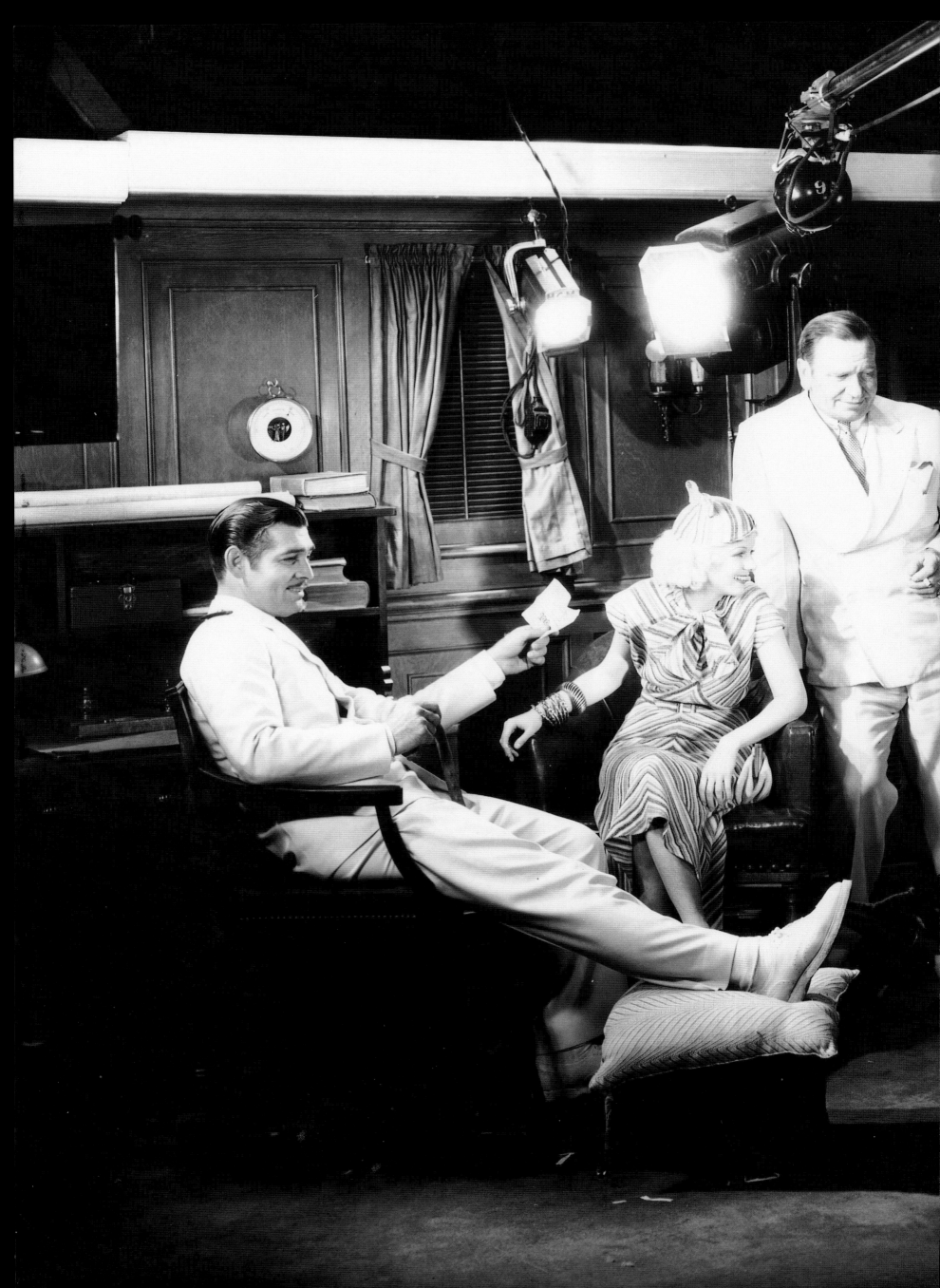

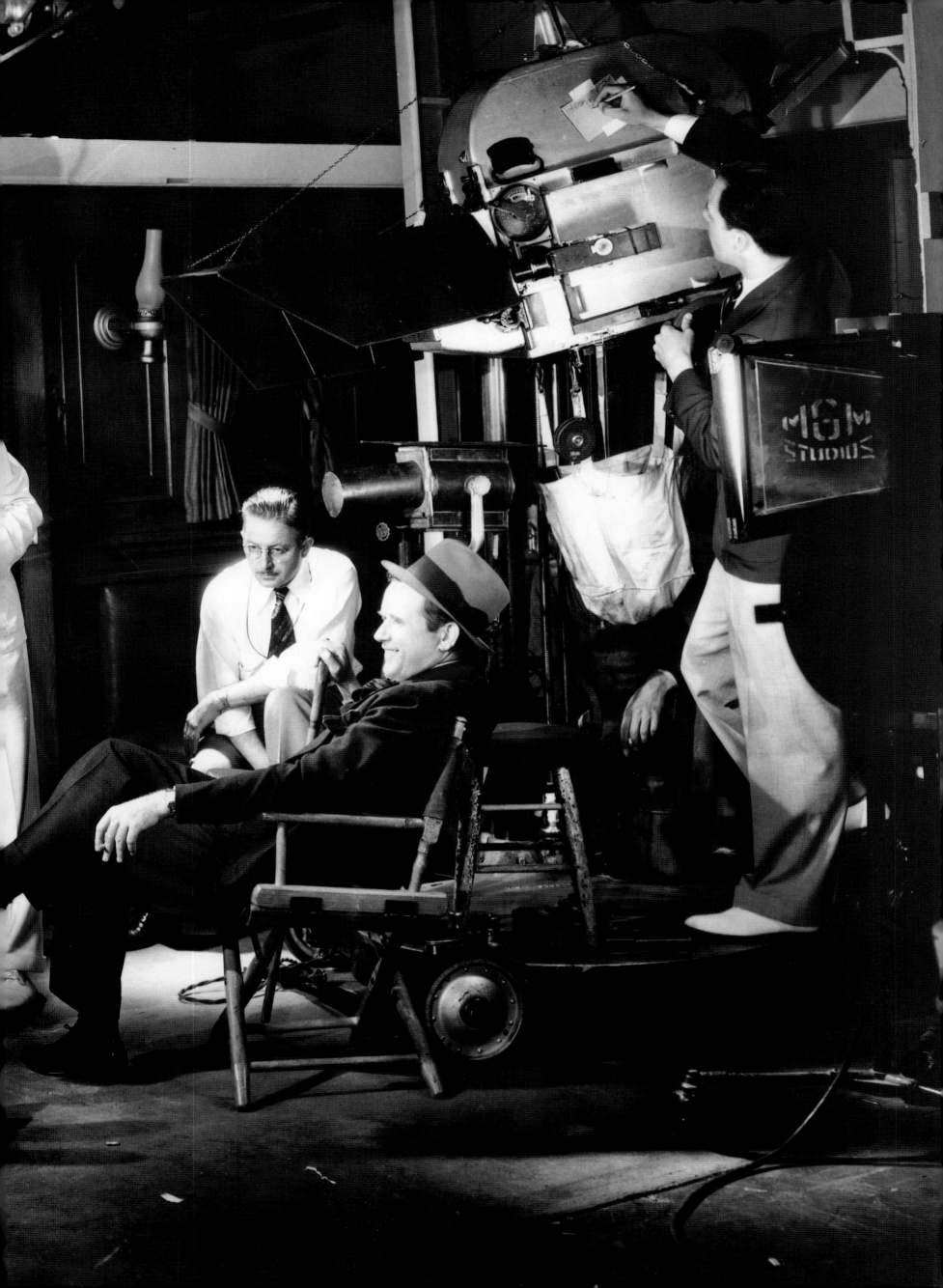

Right: Jack London's classic tale of the Far North, **Call of the Wild** (1935), came to life on the screen with Clark Gable and Loretta Young. Most of the film was made on location at Mt Baker in Washington state, 5000 feet above sea level. It was the highest location ever chosen by Hollywood. Snow ploughs worked day and night over 65 miles to make way for the equipment. Blizzards delayed production, forcing the cast and crew to spend three months on the mountain instead of the anticipated six weeks.

While the two stars were snowbound on Mt Baker, rumors spread through Hollywood that Gable was having an affair with his beautiful leading lady. Later Loretta Young said of him, 'I think every woman he ever met was in love with him.' Her statement was not far from the truth — many of Gable's leading ladies found him irresistible, a feeling shared by women all over the world.

Gable was at the peak of his career. A week after **Call of the Wild** was completed, Gable won his Oscar for **It Happened One Night**. The next five years would be marked by a string of successes — **China Seas**, **Mutiny on the Bounty**, **San Francisco**, **Idiot's Delight**, **Boom Town** and the role of his career — Rhett Butler in **Gone With the Wind**.

Above: In his campaign for City Supervisor, Blackie Norton (Clark Gable) pledges to rid San Francisco's Barbary Coast of its firetrap buildings. **San Francisco** (1936) had it all—Gable, Spencer Tracy, the golden-voiced Jeanette McDonald and stunning special effects recreating the 1906 earthquake.

Facing page: Gable as Jack Thornton, the adventurous prospector in **Call of the Wild** (1935) who loses the woman he loves and finds solace in the wilderness and the companionship of his loyal sled dog, Buck.

Above: Gable was loaned to Warner Bros for a comedy with Marion Davies. **Cain and Mabel** (1936) followed the exploits of a prize fighter named Larry Cain (Clark Gable) and a musical comedy star, Mabel O'Dare (Marion Davies), who stage a wild romance as a publicity stunt.

Facing page: An MGM publicity still of the King of Hollywood.

Above: Offscreen, Jean Harlow visits with Gable and his second wife, Ria.

Facing page: The incomparable team of Gable and Harlow in **Saratoga** (1937), the sixth and last film they made together. During production, Jean Harlow became ill and died of uremic poisoning at the age of 26. MGM immediately announced that out of respect to Harlow the film would not be completed. The studio then reversed its position, rewriting the script so that Harlow's character, now played by Mary Dees, was seen only from the back or from obscured angles. Harlow's voice was dubbed by yet another actress.

Overleaf: The King and Queen of Hollywood (Clark Gable and Myrna Loy) in **Test Pilot** (1938) with Spencer Tracy, the man who first jokingly referred to Gable as the King.

Above: The classic Gable smile that won million of hearts.

Facing page: Much to the delight of audiences, Gable hoofed it up in **Idiot's Delight** (1939). Years later, his 'Puttin' on the Ritz' tap routine was affectionately parodied in Mel Brook's **Young Frankenstein** (1974).

Overleaf: Gable with his **Idiot's Delight** costar, a blonde Norma Shearer.

Above and facing page: Gable once again plays the daredevil in **Too Hot to Handle** (1938) as Chris Hunter, a top cameraman for Union Newsreels. With Alma Harding (Myrna Loy) in tow, Chris heads for the Amazon in search of a story and Alma's missing brother.

Overleaf: Clark Gable in the role for which he is best remembered—Rhett Butler in **Gone With the Wind** (1939). This scene takes place early in the movie, at the Wilkes' family barbecue. While the women are napping, the men have gathered to discuss the topic that is on everyone's mind—war. Charles Hamilton (Rand Brooks) takes the stance of most Southerners—that the South will whip the Yankees in a month. Rhett Butler holds no such illusions and does not hesitate to voice his views, however unpopular they might be.

Clark Gable received top billing and his performance is indelibly etched in the minds and hearts of movie lovers, yet compared to the other key actors Gable spent relatively little time on screen. Part of the credit for Gable's success must be given to director Victor Fleming. Fleming was the ideal director for Gable. Known as a man's director, Fleming had guided Gable through some of his best he-man roles, most notably **Red Dust**. A personal friend as well, Fleming persuaded Gable that Rhett had to weep when Melanie breaks the news of Scarlett's miscarriage. Gable vehemently objected and threatened to walk off the picture, declaring that tears would ruin his image. Fleming induced Gable to shoot the scene both ways, and having done the scene as Fleming wanted Gable was convinced that the director was right.

Above: Rhett urges Melanie (Olivia de Havilland) to tell him where her husband, Ashley (Leslie Howard), has gone, as her sister-in-law India Wilkes (Alicia Rhett) looks on disapprovingly.

Facing page: To those who had read Margaret Mitchell's novel, Clark Gable *was* Rhett Butler. In fact, thousands of letters poured into Selznick International (the production company) demanding that Clark Gable play Rhett Butler. Ironically, Gable had his doubts that he could live up to the public's expectations and suggested that Ronald Colman play the part.

Overleaf: Rhett encounters Scarlett (Vivien Leigh), in her widow's weeds, at the Atlanta Bazaar. Leigh won an Academy Award for Best Actress for her flawless portrayal of Scarlett O'Hara, and Gable was nominated for Best Actor.

In the land of the movie stars, where marriages are all too fleeting, the marriage of Clark Gable and Carole Lombard was declared a match made in heaven. A steady couple for three years, the two eloped to Kingman, Arizona on 29 March 1939, when Clark had a few days break from filming **Gone With the Wind**.

Within twenty-four hours, the newlyweds (*these pages*) were back in Hollywood to meet with the anxious press. Carole was dressed the way Clark liked her best—in an elegant but simply tailored gray flannel suit. She was one of the highest paid female movie stars, but she would gradually devote less time to being a movie star and more time to being Mrs Clark Gable, the perfect wife. The couple hoped to have a child, but that was not to be.

These pages: Gable and Lombard quickly cast aside their movie star personas and settled into life as Mr and Mrs Clark Gable at their ranch in Encino, California. He called her 'Ma,' and she called him 'Pa.' Clark, playing the role of the gentleman farmer, decided to sell fresh eggs and bought six hundred chickens. Carole designed an egg box with a chicken wearing a crown and the logo 'The King's Eggs,' but the chickens didn't cooperate in this venture and the King couldn't deliver his eggs.

With the same fervor she had devoted to her career, Carole devoted herself to taking care of Clark. She became the outdoorsy sort and joined Clark in his favorite pastimes—fishing and hunting. Ever the prankster, marriage did nothing to change her love of the practical joke. She taunted Clark in a way that no one else would have even attempted and Clark adored her for it, for she understood him completely and knew just when to stop teasing. Gable, too, had a keen sense of humor and a rejoinder for every one of her jokes.

Sadly, their happiness was all too brief. In January 1942, Carole Lombard was returning from a war bond drive when her plane crashed into a mountainside, killing everyone on board. A short time later, a bereaved Gable joined the Army, as Carole had asked him to do.

Facing page: **They Met in Bombay** (1941) cast Clark Gable and Rosalind Russell as jewel thieves in pursuit of a fabulous diamond pendent. The two had worked together before in **China Seas** and had a comfortable working relationship. Russell admired Gable's gracefulness, commenting that he handled a love scene with ease. Russell's esteem for Gable extended to Gable's wife, Carole, whom she sent a dozen pairs of hand-stitched leather gloves when filming was completed.

Gable's relationship with his next leading lady provided a marked contrast to the comfort and ease with which he and Rosalind Russell had worked. Gable's love scenes with Lana Turner (*above*) in **Honky Tonk** (1941) sent Carole Lombard scurrying down to the set to keep an eye on things. Much to Carole's dismay, the Gable-Turner combo ignited the screen and studio executives immediately developed a new project for the two sex symbols—**Somewhere I'll Find You** (1942).

Above: Gable was working on the Lana Turner vehicle, **Somewhere I'll Find You** (1942), when Carole Lombard was killed. Production was halted for several weeks, until Gable, ever the professional, insisted that cameras begin rolling again. His sense of discipline got him through his scenes, but after the day's work he hated to return to a home without Carole.

Joan Crawford hated to see her old friend and lover so tormented and offered a sympathetic ear. Gable finally accepted her offer for dinner and talked until three. Until filming was completed, he relied on Crawford's support and went to her house for dinner every evening. Once the film was done, he enlisted in the Army.

The still *on the facing page* is from Crawford and Gable's final film together, **Strange Cargo** (1940).

Clark Gable was sworn into the Army Air Corps as a buck private at a Los Angeles recruiting office on 12 August 1942. He was 41 years old. After attending Officers Candidate School in Miami, Florida, he was shipped overseas with the Eighth Air Force. His official job was to make a training film about aerial gunners. Gable lived up to his screen image and volunteered for five bombing missions over Germany. The photo *above* shows Lieutenant Clark Gable, as a machine gunner, just prior to a bombing raid on the Ruhr Valley in 1943.

When German Air Minister Hermann Goering heard that Gable was in Europe, he added his name to the list of Americans wanted dead or alive. Gable he wanted alive so he could present Hitler with his favorite American movie star.

Shortly before his return to the United States, Captain Gable was awarded the Distinguished Flying Cross and Air Medal. In June 1944, he was promoted to the rank of major and discharged.

Above: Captain Gable consults with Staff Sergeant Kenneth C Huls (left) and Staff Sergeant Philip J Hulse, as they prepare for takeoff for a bombing raid.

Above: An MGM publicity still from the postwar era.

Facing page: Gable's first postwar film was **Adventure** (1945), the story of a hard-boiled sailor who marries a librarian (Greer Garson). MGM proudly announced 'Gable's back and Garson's got him.' The film was a perfect vehicle for Clark Gable, and audiences loved Greer Garson.

Above: Clark Gable chats with a group of fans, American soldiers stationed in London, during the filming of **Never Let Me Go** (1953), which was shot entirely in England. The film was directed by Delmar Daves and produced by Clarence Brown.

A consummate professional, Clark Gable was always nattily attired in a well-cut suit and a white shirt with French cuffs when he appeared in public to meet his fans. Back in 1939, during the filming of **Gone With the Wind**, the director complained about the way Gable's costumes fit him and ordered wardrobe to make sure that Rhett Butler was as well dressed as Clark Gable.

Above: Gene Tierney breaks for lunch, while Clark Gable enjoys a cigarette on location for **Never Let Me Go**. To the right of Gene Tierney are two of the leading feature players, Bernard Miles and Richard Haydn.

Never Let Me Go is the story of Philip Sutherland (Clark Gable), a foreign correspondent, who marries a Russian ballerina (Gene Tierney). He is deported from Russia and forced to leave his wife, Marya Lamarkina, behind.

The boat that provides a convenient lunch spot for the four actors will be used in the scene in which an attempt is made to rescue Marya. Richard Haydn plays the part of the sailor who pilots the boat during the dramatic rendezvous at sea.

Clark Gable appeared with the striking Ava Gardner in three films: **The Hucksters** (1947), **Lone Star** (1952) and **Mogambo** (1953). **The Hucksters** followed on the heels of **Adventure** and to make sure that his next leading lady would not be another Greer Garson, whom he thoroughly disliked, Gable arranged to do a screen test with Ava Gardner before she was signed to the film. She passed with flying colors. Five years later they met again for **Lone Star** (*facing page*), a film about the annexation of Texas.

Their best work together was **Mogambo** (*above*), a remake of **Red Dust**, with Ava Gardner in the Jean Harlow role. Set in Africa, this version features Gable as a great white hunter and Grace Kelly as the young Englishwoman with whom he has an affair. Although **Mogambo** lacked the erotic charge that ignited **Red Dust**, Gable played the part with a natural ease and Grace Kelly received an Oscar nomination for Best Supporting Actress.

Above: Clark Gable and Grace Kelly met on the set of **Mogambo** and immediately formed a close attachment. In a manner reminiscent of Carole Lombard, she called him 'Ba,' which is Swahili for father. While on location in Africa, they went hunting and swimming together. Back in Holly-wood, they were frequent companions, and had it not been for the difference in their ages—he was 52, she 24—they might have married.

Facing page: Though aging, he was still the King, even as his kingdom was dying.

Previous pages: Jane Russell removes a bemused Clark Gable's boots in **The Tall Men**, 1955.

No longer on contract to MGM, Gable was now freelancing and doing quite well. In 1955, he made two movies for Twentieth Century-Fox, **Soldier of Fortune** with Susan Hayward and **The Tall Men** (*these pages*) with Jane Russell. Both were fast-paced action films that revitalized Gable's he-man image. For these two films, he worked for a percentage of the gross, which earned him a fair amount of money.

His personal life had improved as well. On 7 July 1955 he married Kay Williams Spreckels. The two had dated in the early 1940s after Carole's death, but not content as one of Gable's many consorts, she had married sugar magnate Adolph Spreckels Jr. After Gable's divorce from Lady Ashley, he rediscovered Kay, who was now divorced from Spreckels.

The marriage was a happy one. Kay devoted herself to Clark, going hunting, fishing or golfing with him whenever he wanted. Her two children from her previous marriage gave Gable the family he always wanted.

Overleaf: Clark Gable and Cameron Mitchell in **The Tall Men**. They play two Texans, brothers who head to Montana in search of gold.

Left: The fourth release of **Gone With the Wind** in 1954 once again made Clark Gable a top box office draw. More than ever, Gable was firmly entrenched as a Hollywood icon. The rerelease was shortly before Gable's involvement in another film about the antebellum South—**Band of Angels** (1957), which was filmed on location in Louisiana. As had been the case nearly 20 years earlier in Georgia during the filming of **Gone With the Wind**, Mr and Mrs Gable were treated like royalty by the locals. Even Gable's costars, Yvonne DeCarlo and Sidney Portier, were in awe of him.

Comparisons between the two films were inevitable, and the contrast of Gable in his signature role with what is probably the worst role of his career was jarring. Gable had worked successfully with **Band of Angels** director Raoul Walsh in **The Tall Men** (1955), but their subsequent collaborations, **The King and Four Queens** (1956) and **Band of Angels**, were dismal affairs. In **Band of Angels**, Raoul Walsh tried to make Gable's character of Hamish Bond as much like Rhett Butler as possible, the end result being that Gable ends up a caricature of himself. Fortunately, Gable's reputation far outweighed the ill effects of **Band of Angels** and he is remembered for his classic portrayal of Rhett Butler rather than for this embarrassment.

Above: In the late 1950s, Clark Gable signed with Paramount for three comedies: **Teacher's Pet** (*above*) with Doris Day (1958), **But Not for Me** with Carroll Baker (1959) and **It Started in Naples** (1960) with Sophia Loren. Lightweight and amusing, all three demonstrated that Gable still had a flair for comedy.

Facing page: Clark Gable's popularity endured for thirty years — an accomplishment realized by only a few of Hollywood's stars.

While working on **It Started in Naples**, producer Frank
Taylor contacted Clark Gable about playing the leading
man, Gay Langland, in playwright Arthur Miller's **The Misfits**, which he had written especially for his wife, Marilyn
Monroe. Taylor later recalled, 'I knew only one actor in the
world who could express the essence of complete masculinity and virility that we needed for the leading role. And
that was Clark Gable.'

Gable read the script and although he liked it, he didn't
understand the character of Gay, for the part was far more
cerebral than any role he had ever played. Gable met with
Arthur Miller to discuss the part and realized that Gay was
a man very much like himself. He agreed to do the part and
his performance was hailed by many as the finest of his
career.

Above: A group portrait of the cast and crew of **The
Misfits** (1961): producer Frank Taylor (under the ladder),
playwright Arthur Miller (top), Eli Wallach (in front of Miller), director John Huston (next to Wallach), Montgomery
Clift (bottom row, left), Marilyn Monroe and Clark Gable.

Above: **The Misfits** was the final film for both Marilyn Monroe and Clark Gable. Emotionally, Marilyn Monroe was in fragile condition when filming began. Her marriage to Arthur Miller deteriorating, she relied on alcohol and sleeping pills to cope and consequently was always late for work and had trouble remembering her lines. Some days she never showed up at all. Monroe would begin one more movie after **The Misfits**, but would die of a drug overdose before it was completed.

Gable treated Marilyn with compassion, but her erratic behavior was nevertheless stressful on him as well as on everyone else involved in the project. **The Misfits** was equally draining physically. Though Gable was 59, he insisted on doing his own stunts in the dessert heat. Two days after filming was completed, Clark Gable suffered a heart attack. He died on 16 November 1960. On 20 March 1961, the son he had longed for was born to his wife, Kay.

These pages: For 30 years Clark Gable reigned as the undisputed King of Hollywood Gable, first as the dashing young actor and then as the mature and ruggedly handsome leading man.

GABLE-Metro-Goldwyn-Mayer

MG42401

Filmography

STAGE PERFORMANCES

What Price Glory? *(1925)*

Machinal *(1928)*

Love, Honor and Betray *(1930)*

The Last Mile *(1930)*

FILMS

Forbidden Paradise *(1924, Silent; extra)*
The Pacemakers *(1925, Silent; extra)*
The Merry Widow *(1925, Silent; extra)*
The Plastic Age *(1925; extra)*
North Star *(1926; extra)*
The Painted Desert *(1931)*
The Easiest Way *(1931)*
Dance, Fools, Dance *(1931)*
The Secret Six *(1931)*
The Finger Points *(1931)*
Laughing Sinners *(1931)*
A Free Soul *(1931)*
Night Nurse *(1931)*
Sporting Blood *(1931)*
Susan Lenox: Her Fall and Rise *(1931)*
Possessed *(1931)*
Hell Divers *(1931)*
Polly of the Circus *(1932)*
Red Dust *(1932)*
Strange Interlude *(1932)*
No Man of Her Own *(1932)*
The White Sister *(1933)*
Hold Your Man *(1933)*
Night Flight *(1933)*
Dancing Lady *(1933)*
It Happened One Night *(1934)*
Men In White *(1934)*
Manhattan Melodrama *(1934)*
Chained *(1934)*
Forsaking All Others *(1934)*
After Office Hours *(1935)*
Call of the Wild *(1935)*
China Seas *(1935)*
Mutiny on the Bounty *(1935)*
Wife Versus Secretary *(1936)*
San Francisco *(1936)*

Cain and Mabel *(1936)*
Love on the Run *(1936)*
Parnell *(1937)*
Saratoga *(1938)*
Test Pilot *(1938)*
Too Hot to Handle *(1938)*
Idiot's Delight *(1939)*
Gone With the Wind *(1939)*
Strange Cargo *(1940)*
Boom Town *(1940)*
Comrade X *(1940)*
They Met in Bombay *(1941)*
Honky Tonk *(1941)*
Somewhere I'll Find You *(1942)*
Adventure *(1945)*
The Hucksters *(1947)*
Homecoming *(1948)*
Command Decision *(1948)*
Any Number Can Play *(1949)*
Key to the City *(1950)*
To Please a Lady *(1950)*
Across the Wide Missouri *(1951)*
Callaway Went Thataway *(1951)*
Lone Star *(1952)*
Never Let Me Go *(1953)*
Mogambo *(1953)*
Betrayed *(1954)*
Soldier of Fortune *(1955)*
The Tall Men *(1955)*
The King and Four Queens *(1956)*
Band of Angels *(1957)*
Run Silent, Run Deep *(1958)*
Teacher's Pet *(1958)*
But Not For Me *(1959)*
It Started in Naples *(1960)*
The Misfits *(1961)*

Index

Page 112: A Clarence Bull portrait of Clark Gable. 'From the photographer's point of view,' Bull later recalled, 'it was easy to shoot Gable because he was so natural. He didn't try to give you static, dry poses. He'd just move and try different things. He could always tell when he struck a pose or expression that was good.'